A Moving Train

Know Who You Are

*Inspirational Poems, Prayers and Musical
Lyrics to revive your Spirit*

FYNE C. OGONOR

Copyright © 2021 by Fyne Ogonor.
www.FyneOgonor.com
fyneauthor@gmail.com

Library of Congress Control Number: 2021930909

ISBN: Hardcover 978-1-951460-18-1

      Softcover 978-1-951460-19-8

      eBook 978-1-951460-20-4

Revised & Expanded Second Edition

All rights reserved. No part of this book may be reproduced or transmitted in any form or by any means, electronic or mechanical, including photocopying, recording, or by any information storage and retrieval system, without permission in writing from the copyright owner.

First © 2017 by Fyne C. Ogonor.
Library of Congress Control Number: 2016911877

Atlanta, Georgia, USA
www.ronvalinternational.com

I dedicate this book, *A Moving Train*, to the Almighty God, for making this project possible.

I also dedicate this book to you reading this book. May you receive clarity on your identity-who you really are, and let the purpose of your being manifest, so you'll experience a joy-filled life.

Contents

08	Introduction
10	Almighty God, I Thank You for Today
11	My Earnest Plea!
12	Stand Up for the Right!
14	The Echoes of Life
16	The Wings of Heaven
18	God the Designer
19	Night Rest
20	Heavenly Gaze
21	A Moving Train
23	Accept Me as I Am
24	Dream!!
26	I Must Achieve!
28	The Favor of God
30	God's Presence!

34	Be Not Afraid! God's Got Your Back
35	Jesus Christ, My Leader
36	An Ordered Step
37	Heaven Be My Home
38	I Kneel on My Knees
40	My Destiny
42	Personalized Victory Prayer
43	Thank You, Lord!
44	Gratitude!
45	The Covenant
46	Let God Arise!
47	All I Have, I Give to You
48	My Feelings Today
49	I Know My Lord Is Able
51	It's Not Over Until God Says It's Over
52	Epilogue: The Author
55	Acknowledgements
56	References

Introduction

Do You Know You?

A Moving Train is more than a poetry book. This book is composed of Inspirational Poems, Prayers, and Musical Lyrics, to strengthen your Faith and Points You to Hope.

It is a roadmap to living a blissful life; starting with the identification of your real self, discovering your mission, and following the prescribed roadmap in the journey of life to ensure your arrival at your destination.

Life is reality, but to fulfill your mission on earth, you must dream, and dream big. Then, follow your dream—you've got what it takes. You're all you need; with the roadmap in your hand provided to you by your creator in the beginning of life, you cannot fail, but to achieve. Is life what you make of it? Or is life really the acceptance of what has already been ordained for you?

Make your dream big enough for God to use and enlarge for His purpose. Do not share your dream with the dream killers: the little minds, the pessimists, and those with impure hearts. Rather, focus on what your creator says about you: "You're wonderfully made", highly favored, the apple of His eyes, His beloved, a praise to God, a daughter/son of the Most High God, and a friend to the great Shepherd, the High Priest, the 'All'.

Almighty God, I thank You For Today!

Morning Prayer of Adoration

Almighty God, I thank You for today.
Morning has come for me to start my journey.
Let Your presence be with me wherever I go.
Wherever life's journey takes me today,
May Your footsteps go before me.
Allow my thoughts to be guided by your purpose for me.
Let my tongue speak forth thy praise.
At the end of today, may all glory, honor, and
adoration be yours only;
Through Christ Jesus, my Savior's name. Amen.

My Earnest Plea!

Give me the strength O Lord!
To do the things I have to do.
Give me the Courage to run
The extra mile to get to my destination.
Give me an open mind
To see and tackle things objectively.
Give me a level eye,
Knowledge to understand,
And wisdom to act and react wisely.
Thank You, Lord, for Thy blessings.
Amen.

Stand up for the Right!

Stand up for the right!
Who you are is not a deterrent; stand up for the right.
Put the wrong to shame, by standing up for the right.
When the wrong tries to silence your voice, shout louder
for the listening ears of the world to hear.
And their mouth shall speak forth to silence the wrong.

When your hands and legs are shackled up,
mourn and wail in the open.
The heads of humans in the world must turn,
so their eyes can see.
And their mouth must proclaim, nay! Nay!
For the wrong should not prevail.
When the eyes of the world see,
the voice of judgement must be heard.
The wrongs that the eyes of the world see,
must be condemned in the open.
Who can stand the judgement of the world?
Only a lost soul, who will be judged in the
highest court of heaven.
While standing for the right, remember to
invite peace into your heart.

The best way to fight the wrong, is to
invite peace into your heart.
Allow the Almighty God to fight for you,
and victory shall definitely be yours.
Therefore, stand up!
Stand against the wrong; stand for peace.
Stand! Stand up for your right; but stand with God.

The Echoes of Life

Standing in the middle of the universe seeking
the meaning of life,
I silently listen to the echoes of the world;
I heard two distinct voices expressing the meaning of life.
From the distorted heart, I heard:
Life is hopeless, full of disappointments and heartache.
Life is worries, doubt, fear, and anxiety.
Life is depressing, hateful, ugly, wickedness, and unfair.
Life is imperfect, full of brokenness, weeping, agony, and crying.
Life is natural, disasters, and destruction.
Life is begging, chasing, and hunting.
Life is learning, filled with illusions, unorganized and emotional.
Life is approval, seeking, heartbeat, and music.
Life is a journey, filled with drama and uncertainty.

From the blissful heart, I heard:
Life is hopeful, believing, and trusting.
Life is good, full of assurance.
Life is graceful, loving, cherishing, and full of happiness.
Life is beautiful, lively, and blissful.
Life is living, spiritual, and inward.
Life is sacrifice, giving, encouraging, and receiving.

Life is application, testing and result.
Life is reality, certainty, and melody.
Life is a destination, supernatural, and eternal.
In the end, I realized, helped by wisdom, that the world's echoes of
life are not the meaning of life.
Rather, they are mere expressions of life.
Definition of life through the eyes of the world projects:
Life is whatever you want it to mean to you;
Because life comes with a gift of choice.
And, every situation comes with a timeline;
For nothing really lasts forever.
What is life in reality?
Life is knowing your identity, foundation, and your heritage.
In essence, life is knowing who you are, and to whom you belong.
Life is discovering your assignment;
And aligning your assignment with your dream,
To fulfill the purpose established by your Creator.
Life is setting no boundary to how high you can climb.
Life is knowing you exist because of others.
You're sent to earth not by yourself, and not for yourself.
You're here to fulfill a mission; a mission specifically
for a group of people.
Without you, their lives would not be fulfilled.
And without whom, your mission can never be accomplished.
Therefore, avail yourself, commune, embrace, love, care,
And let your kindness be a candlelight in their hearts.
Rejoice, cherish, and celebrate life together;
in the name of Yahweh.
Life is gracious, freedom, victory, hope, and eternal.

The Wings of Heaven

In a trance of a moment, I see the wings of heaven descending to earth.
In the cloud of glory comes the crowd of wings floating
down from heaven.
I hear the trumpet blowing loud and clear.
The skeletons in the earth rising from shore to shore.
In a glaring vision, the skeletons turned to clear glassy flesh.
I inquired in the spirit, and I knew they were bodies
of heavenly bound saints
Rising proclaiming hosanna to the King.
Ascending to meet the Lord in the cloud with a shout of acclamation:
Blessed be the Name of our Lord Jehovah, Yahweh; the Lion of Judah.
He shall reign and reign forever.
Blessed be the King of glory;
Our Messiah, Lord Jesus, the Christ.
A gaze at the wings of heaven, I see that the wings are heavenly angels,
Descending with the Lion of Judah, our Savior, Redeemer-King.
Now I know this is the return of my King, my Savior,
Lord Jesus, the Christ.

The King of kings and the Lord of lords, standing in the clouds of heaven
receiving His Saints with these greetings:
Welcome home, well-done, you good and faithful servants.

I woke from the trance of a moment, the picture of my vision remained in my memory.

As I thought of my vision, I suddenly understood the meaning of my trance of a moment.

And I knew it was a warning to us all people on earth of our Lord soon returning King.

Take heed, people of the world, what we know from the holy book, the bible, must surely come to pass.

The day of reckoning is unknown, the bible warns us.

What I know for sure, the day, the hour, is fast approaching.

Why wait, why delay, why not now?

I mean for you to come home.

The Lord is watching, calling, and waiting.

Come home my child, come home!

You may have fallen short of my glory, come to me, my child.

I, the Lord your King, still love you anyhow.

Blessed are those who hear, and obey the word of God, written in the holy book, the bible.

God the Designer

God the Designer,
The Creator of heaven and earth.
On earth all things were created by Him.
"Unto thee O Lord I lift up my soul."
Bring out the light in me to shine and give light
to the whole world.
Like the sun by day, and like the bright moon by night.
And let my sojourn move like the stars.

Night Rest

In peace I lay me down now to sleep.
God let me wake up in the morning with joy.
And let Thy glory shine in me now, and forever. Amen.

Heavenly Gaze

Prayer of Confidence

In the midst of the clouds I gazed up in the heavens to seek
the face of my God.
Down below is full of distress, calamities upon calamities;
I refuse to look down because I know my help comes
only from above.
The giants below hound me and did everything to pull me down.
But I refuse to look down because I hear my Lord calling for me;
And I know that my help will come only from above.
The dinosaurs of earth threaten to devour me,
But I must not be afraid.
I am covered with the blood of Jesus.
I am protected by the highest power under and above the universe.
I belong to Jesus Christ.
I will continually praise His name 'till the dawn of the day.
Therefore Lord Jesus,
Adjoin my heart with Thee,
For there's no other way for me but Thine.
Amen.

A Moving Train

A moving Train makes a hell of noise,
Even a deaf person standing by the railroad
Will know that the train is coming.
When people invest their valuable time talking about you,
You are a moving Train.

A moving Train does not identify with the environmental ambience;
Because its own noise overshadows the noise within its surroundings.
A moving Train has no ears to the back, its focus is on its destination.
Every moving Train has a destination.

A Moving Train

When you see a moving Train, clear the way.
A moving Train is like a season,
Nobody can stand in its way.
If you dare, you'll be crushed!

You, the moving Train, close your ears.
You cannot hide your noise,
Just keep moving.

It does not matter the color of smoke from your tail pipe.
Your destination should be your focus;
And success shall definitely be yours.
Thank God for your status,
'A moving Train'.

Accept me as I am

Accept me as I am;
Make no false story.
Know the real me,
Then testify of me
While I'm alive to hear it.
But if you know nothing about me,
Say nothing of me to anyone.
Just accept me as an honor to God.

Dream

Dream! is as big as you can imagine it.
Dream big, and achieve big.
Small dreams limit your success;
Bigger dreams widen your vision, and expand your knowledge.
Dream it, and you can imagine it.
Imagine it, and you can perceive it.
Visualize it, and you can achieve it.
Achievement is success, and success is progress.
Progress begets recognition, acceptance, and visibility.
Dreaming the big dreams is honorable.

A life without a purpose is not worth living. And a life without a dream is **wasted**. Keep on dreaming, and pursue your **dreams** with every bone in your body. In **all** your worldly endeavors, remember, "God first."

I must Achieve!

Nothing will slow me down!
And nothing will stop me.
I must achieve!
I may be in clutches,
But my brain is not.
Handicap is not an excuse.

My physical challenge cannot deter my achievement.
My goal in life must be achieved.
I must climb the highest mountain.
I must jump the deepest valley.
I aim at touching the sky.
Though the negative forces of the world
many times try to pull me down,
But I, must achieve!

My quest to achieve, my honest and humble determination
of my inner self magnets me above and beyond, to connect
with the supreme Almighty.
I, must achieve!

I dedicate this poem, "I Must Achieve" to all the handicapped staff members that served under me, and all my disabled students and pupils over the years. It's been a privilege knowing and serving you. You have influenced my life positively; and I hope I have done the same for you. Hold on to the word of God. There's no handicap in the kingdom of our heavenly Father.

"Let not mercy and truth forsake you;
Bind them around your neck,
Write them on the tablet of your heart,
And so find favor and high esteem
In the sight of God and man.
Trust in the Lord with all your heart,
And lean not on your own understanding;
In all your ways acknowledge Him,
And He shall direct your paths."
Proverbs 3: 3-6 NKJV

With God's favor, you can achieve anything. **Philippians 4:13 says, "I can do all things through Christ who strengthens me."** With faith, we must believe that **"all things are possible with God"** (Matthew 19:26). When the gracious hand of God is in our lives, we experience the favor of God. God's favor opens the right doors for us to succeed in our life endeavors beyond our expectations.

The important thing is that we must believe, have confidence and trust in our God, the Almighty; and have the boldness to be in His presence, praising and thanking Him for His goodness. We must form the habit of expressing our gratitude to our heavenly Father always. Then ask Him anything in the name of our Savior Jesus Christ, and He shall pour His favor in our lives generously because He is a God that never fails His promises. The more we testify of God's goodness, the more of His blessings we shall receive.

Affirmation of Faith

God's presence is always with me.
My being matters to God!
He was in my yesterday during my dark and bright moments.
Yesterday was full of memories good and bad;
But I'm glad it's over.
I arrived today with great expectations, hope, and enthusiasm.
Though the path is filled with challenges, troubles, and temptations;
I will not be afraid, nor be discouraged.
Even in a strong wind,
I will trust my God.
Wherever the wind carries me,
I know God's hands will be there to catch me.
Although I cannot see tomorrow from here,
But one thing I know for sure is that when I get there,
My Lord will still be there waiting for me.
God's presence is always with me.

My brothers and sisters in the Lord, are you going through something and wonder, "where is God?" You feel abandoned and neglected, even rejected?

Do you remember the story of Daniel in the lions' den? God loves Daniel His servant so much that He could have stopped him from being thrown into the lions' den, but He didn't. However, He protected Daniel by putting the lions to sleep.

What about the three Hebrew men, Shadrach, Meshach, and Abednego? God didn't stop their enemies from throwing them into the furnace of fire. But instead of them burning in the fire, God turned the heat in the fire to air conditioning. Their enemies saw a fourth person in the fire, Christ Jesus, the Son of God Himself.

Let's talk about the crucifixion. Jesus the Christ had the power to prevent His enemies from torturing Him. But He didn't because the word of God had to be fulfilled, so you and I could be saved, sanctified from all our impurities, and could overcome the power of sin.

We children of God must at a certain point in our lives experience tribulations. The important thing is, do we know who our God really is? Do we believe, trust, and have faith in Him? If yes, then we should know that He is always there to rescue us.

If God chooses not to deliver you from whatever storm or challenges you are facing, just know that He's still there for you and stay in faith. He will allow you to go through the storm to lead you to a greater testimony.

Therefore, what is your test now shall become your testimony tomorrow. As a child of God, remember that the winds and the storms are never meant to push you down; rather, they are meant to push you forward. Hence, in all situations, we need to glorify God, and stay in faith. Joyce Meyer in one of her telecasts says: "Do not permit yourself to be fearful. Hold your peace and God will fight for you."

Sometimes the storms and winds in our lives are meant to relocate or push us to our destiny to better serve our Godly purpose. On June 14, 2007 Cece Winans in a telecast interview said, "God can use you anywhere, but you have to be where God wants you to be."

When we remove ourselves from God's presence, we have difficulty hearing God's voice. And even when we hear, we don't understand or we simply just don't listen. And for the fact that God loves us so much, He gives us uncountable chances to repent. He'd allow the storms and winds in our lives to wake us up and push us to the destination where He needs us to be to better fulfill His divine purpose in our lives; to accomplish our designated assignment in this universe.

Furthermore, we sometimes face storms not because we are doing something wrong, rather, it is because we are doing something right.

God will not allow you to go through a storm if it will destroy you, or keep you from your destiny. Trust God and let the wind blow you to where God wants you to be. The wind that is meant to destroy you, He can cause it to move you forward for greater testimony.

> Trust God and let the wind blow you to where God wants you to be. The wind that is meant to destroy you, He can cause it to move you forward for greater testimony.

Be not afraid! God's got your back

"Then the word of the Lord came to me saying: "Before I formed you in the womb, I knew you; Before you were born, I sanctified you; And I ordained you a prophet to the nations."
Then said I:
"Ah Lord God!
Behold I cannot speak, for I am a youth."
But the Lord said to me:
"Do not say, 'I am a youth,'
For you shall go to all to whom I send you,
And whatever I command you, you shall speak.
Do not be afraid of their faces,
For I am with you to deliver you," says the Lord."
Jeremiah 1:4-8 NKJV

Jesus Christ My Leader

Prayer of Assurance

The Lord is my Protector and my Provider,
I will never lack.
He provides for me abundantly.
He gives me water from the fountain of life that
pours water unceasingly,
So I will never be thirsty.
He shows me the right path to follow.
Even though my enemies are all around me,
I am not afraid because He is with me.
Your grace and mercy encourages me.
You lift me up above my enemies;
You give me the understanding of the word to speak it with power.
In Your name, God's favor and anointing shall be mine,
And I will serve the Lord forever. Amen.
- Inspired by Psalm 23

An Ordered Step

An ordered step, I request from You, Lord!
You are the only one I want to listen to.
The world is full of discouragement, anguish, and pain.
But I am convinced that You are on my side.
Help me Lord, not to depart from Your presence.
An ordered step, I request from You.

O God when You speak to me,
Turn the volume up so I can hear You.
When You speak, put conviction in my heart to know
You are the one.
Give me understanding to know what You say to me.
Then lead the way, so I can follow.

Sometimes I hear a still voice in my heart,
I wondered is it You Lord, speaking to me?
Or is it just my heart wondering on facts of life?
Dear Lord, speak to me, and
Let me recognize Your voice.
So there'll be no doubt in my heart,
You're leading my way.

Heaven be My Home

O God my Father, stretch Your hands for me.
I have no place in this world.
Please, make heaven my home.
Out of the blue the devil tried to put a stain on my name,
My Blessed name from above.
The accusation spread like a wildfire;
I said to my Lord, "Plead my cause,"
And say to my soul,
"I am your salvation."
I will trust in the shelter of your wings.
Oh please, Lord, make heaven my home.

"Hear my cry, O God;
Attend to my prayer."
Until the end of the earth,
I will cry to you when my heart is overwhelmed just like now.
"Lead me to the Rock that is higher than I"
And be always a shelter for me.
"I will trust in the shelter of your wings"
For You, O God, I give my vows.
Father, You promised to be there for me; For You are my Lord and
my Savior. Please my Savior, make heaven my home.
- Inspired by Psalm 35:1, 3; Psalm 61

I kneel on my Knees

I kneel on my knees,
And poured my heart to God.
Show me Thy way, and teach me how to walk in Thy footsteps.
You said I should knock,
You will open the door for me.
And if I ask, You will give it to me.
Lord, I want You to give me the water from the rock.
I need to live, and live forever.

Jesus my Savior, calls me by my name,
And offers me the water from the rock.
The water to cleanse me as pure as crystal.
The water to quench my thirst, and makes me holy.
Jesus my Rock of Ages cleft for me now!
On my knees I'll worship thee forever. Amen.

> When I cast all my worries and burdens unto my Lord, miracles happen. In other words, when you fight your battles on your knees, the heavenly gate opens. **With the Almighty on your side, you'll win** all the time.

My Destiny

I must fulfill my destiny.
I must go beyond the sky,
To receive my defined destiny.
No devil or enemy can stop me.
My life was supremely designed by the superpower
above the universe.
No power below has authority over me;
Because I am heavenly created and anointed.
Come rain, sun, or dew,
I must live to fulfill my destiny, which was specially
packaged for me before I was born.
Thank you, Lord, for loving me the way you do.

If what you're doing is a God-called destiny, do not allow anything whatsoever to discourage you. It is the job of the devil to challenge the dreams of the children of God. However, from experience, I know that whatever dream God has planted in an individual believing that God, the Almighty is in control, must definitely be fulfilled, no matter the challenges along the way.

Remain faithful to God no matter what. Don't allow your unfavorable circumstances to discourage you. Don't quit on God—be like Joseph. Obedient Joseph did not quit trusting God even when his situation was not favorable. He refused allowing his circumstances to prevent him from serving his Lord our God. (Genesis 39: 1-5).

Our Lord Jesus Christ did not quit on the cross; he endured the pain so we can be redeemed of our sins.

No matter how difficult and painful a situation is, even onto death, in every situation, stay obedient and faithful to our Jehovah, and definitely He will come through for you. You can always count on our God because He never fails.

Prayer of Confidence

Personalized Victory Prayer

"You are my King, O God;"
Command victories for me/us(or insert name).
Through you _____ will push down enemies;
Through your name _____ will trample those who rise
up against _____. "For I will not trust in my bow,
Nor shall my sword save me."
But You have saved _____ from _____ enemies,
And have put to shame those who hated _____.
In God _____ boast all day long,
"And praise Your name forever." Amen.
Psalm 44:4-8

Thank you, Lord!

Thank You, Lord !
God, I feel Your power in me.
You won the battle again for me, and
I thank you for fighting my battles.
You are worthy to be praised.
I have strength in You.
Thank You, my precious Lord!
For Your grace, mercy, and blessings.
Amen.

Gratitude

*Worship Our Lord God
with Thanksgiving.*

"Make a joyful shout to God, all the earth!
Sing out the honor of His name;
Make His praise glorious.
Say to God,
How awesome are Your works!
Through the greatness of Your power Your enemies
shall submit themselves to You.
All the earth shall worship You
And sing praises to You;
They shall sing praises to Your name." Amen.
Psalms 66: 1-4 NKJV

The Covenant

"I will love You O Lord, my strength.
The Lord is my rock, my fortress and my deliverer;
My God, my strength,
In Whom I will trust;
My shield and the horn of my salvation, My stronghold.
I will call upon the Lord,
Who is worthy to be praised;
So shall I be saved from my enemies."
Psalm 18:1-3 NKJV

Let God Arises!

Let God arise! And let His enemies be scattered.
Let all who hate Him be without His presence.
Behold the righteous, be glad, and rejoice before our God.
Sing Praises to our God. Let's sing praises to our God.
Rejoice and be glad, for our Lord is the Almighty;
The Great and Mighty, Father of all.

Sing Praises to God! He is in His holy temple.
Blessed be the Lord, the God of our Salvation,
Who provides us with all reaches and wealth,
Let's glorify His name. Sing Praises and rejoice,
Let's sing praises and rejoice. Glorify our Lord;
For He is the King of Kings and the Lord of Lords.

Blessed be the Lord! The God of our salvation!
"A Father of the fatherless, a defender of widows".
You, oh God! sent a plentiful rain, in the wilderness for Your people.
The Lord gave the word; Our Lord gave the living word.
Our God dwells among us. Blessed be to our Lord.
The creator of heaven and earth, and all therein.
Amen.
Inspired by Psalm 68.

All I have I give to you

All I am, and all I have,
I give to You my Lord.
I give to You because all is Yours.
I give back to You O Lord,
All I am, and all I have,
I receive from You, my God.
With a gladdened heart,
I return to You what You own.
Accept all I am, and all I give,
For I give to You, in the name of Jesus.
All I am, and all I have,
I give to You my Jesus.
I give to You
Because You blessed me with it.
Your gift at Calvary to me,
I cannot repay.
But I bring to You
My heart of Love;
Because You first loved me.
Take all I am, and all I have.
I give to You, my Love;
My Savior Jesus.

My Feelings Today

Today must be embraced in all entirety.
Every moment lived, seen, and felt must always be remembered.
I wish to forgive the wrongs of today,
But all views of today will never be forgotten.
For it is stamped in the memories of those who lived it.
Behold! I bid you to stamp the picture of today in your heart,
so it won't elude you.
Vision the picture of today and make it right.
For when tomorrow arrives,
The picture today becomes permanent.
Though the seasons change,
But Our God remains the same.

I know my Lord is able

The salvation of the Almighty
Is upon my life; and
I know my Lord is able
To carry me through.
In God I trust, for He is
My refuge, and my fortress.
Therefore, I know He's able to carry me through.

In the lonely wilderness,
My God is with me for company.
In the dark places of trials,
In the valley, on the mountain top,
I am not afraid; because,
My God is my light.
And I know He is able to carry me through.

My Father's promise!
When I depend on Him:
No evil shall befall me,
Nor shall any plague come
near my dwelling.

When I trip and stumble,
His Angels will catch me,
Lest I dash my foot against a stone;
Because He is always able to carry me through

I shall tread and trample under my foot,
The lion and the cobra and I shall not be hurt.
My God promised to deliver me
From all troubles; because,
He is able to carry me through.
O yes! I know for certain,
My God is able to carry me through.

It's not over until God say it's over

It's not over until God says it's over!
I am created by my heavenly Father.
I came to this world not by accident.
He designed my life just right,
To serve my purpose on earth.
I say the devil has no right to touch my life.
Get thee behind me Satan,
You have no right!
No right to my life.
I am covered with the blood of Jesus Christ.

Heaven declares war against my enemies.
Touch not my anointed my God declares.
He designed every step of my life pathway.
He sent His beloved son to wash away my sins.
Every day I live and feel gloriously and victoriously.
Thank You Father, for sending me to planet earth.
I'll see You at the end of my assignment on earth.
Heaven! Heaven is my permanent home.
I love You Oh Lord, my All.

Epilogue

The Author

Evang. Fyne C. Ogonor was born and brought up in Rivers State, Nigeria. After high school, she traveled to the United States of America, where she obtained her Bachelor of Arts degree with honors from Huston-Tillotson University in Austin, Texas. She later earned a dual Executive MBA degree in Management and Marketing from Mercer University in Atlanta, Georgia, USA. After that, she took an interest in the educational field, and she delved into research and self-training in educational institution management and administration. Fyne had a burning desire to make a difference in humanity, especially to ensure that every child is given an opportunity and encouraged to be all he/she can be, in spite of the child's personality, social or economic background.

Also, she believes children should be taught to learn how to learn, to know how to take advantage of every privilege afforded to them, and should be given an opportunity to practice self-accountability and responsibility at an early age. Doing so will help children to inculcate self-discipline and higher measures of integrity and to display a high moral standard in their communities as decent leaders and citizens of our societies. Moreover, they will showcase model behaviors to those behind them, as they live positively and with gratitude. This inclination led Fyne to take action by becoming an advocate for children and youths. As a result, she founded an educational institute in 2004 where she felt she could make a difference by exercising her philanthropical role to the pupils and students in her community.

After her tertiary education, Fyne successfully excelled in her profession, business management and marketing, and climbed the American corporate ladder. She later established her own businesses, both in the USA and in Nigeria. However, in light of her call to the Lord's vineyard, she moved to Nigeria temporarily in 2008.

In addition to her corporate American achievements in management and administration, while in Nigeria, she also made an impact in leading people in enhancing the existence of humanity. She held the chairmanship position for two local governments in Rivers State for five years in the Nigerian Association of Proprietors of Private Schools (NAPPS).

Furthermore, in addition to her Children and Youth Ministries, the Lord expanded her horizon into women ministries. At the moment, her ministerial services cover both West Africa and the USA, but she hopes to expand to other parts of the world in the near future.

For now, she's expanding to other parts of the world through her published books, online mentoring, and coaching. And especially, the Lord is using her mightily through her ministerial services in counseling and praying for all whom God sends her way. The Almighty God is working tremendously through her, bringing hope to the hopeless. The barren have children, the sick are healed, the troubled hearts are comforted, and prayers are answered. Her teaching focuses on love, faith, hope, obedience, and gratitude. In a nutshell, she is an ambassador with the message of knowing and understanding our special selves, our spiritual identity, and the why of our existence on planet earth.

Evang. Fyne C. Ogonor, is an inspirational and motivational speaker, a seasoned entrepreneur, philanthropist, business consultant, and a spiritual counselor, and a song writer who loves singing. She is married and blessed with five children. She's also the author of the following books:

My Pledge! The Power of Prayer; Discover Your Coat of Many Colors: You Were Born to Be Significant; the Baby Eagle and the Chicks series; and The Best Gift Ever: A Letter From God at Christmas.

Acknowledgements

I want to thank my daughter, Valerie for typesetting some of this script, and for being there for me always.

I also thank all Ronval International team members: editors, illustrators, and designers who participated in the completion of this project. May God bless us all in Jesus' Name. Amen.

All glory and adoration I give to my Lord for the inspired words He'd given me through the Holy Spirit. I especially thank God for assuring me with promises I can always count on, because He is always able to carry me through.

A Moving Train

Biblical References

Proverbs 3:3-6 NKJV
Philippians 4:13 NKJV
Matthew 19:26
Jeremiah 1:4-8 NKJV
Psalm 23 inspired
Psalm35:1, 3; Psalm 61 inspired
Psalm 44:4-8 NKJV
Psalm 66:1-4 inspired
Psalm 18:1-3 NKJV
Psalm 91 inspired
Psalm 68, Inspired